T0113603

IF JESUS IS THE ANSWER, WHAT IS THE QUESTION?

Questions from God

James J. Genova, PhD

WESTBOW
P R E S S®
A DIVISION OF THOMAS NELSON
& ZONDERVAN

Scripture taken from the Holy Bible, NEW INTERNATIONAL VERSION®.
Copyright © 1973, 1978, 1984, 2011 by Biblica, Inc. All rights reserved worldwide.
Used by permission. NEW INTERNATIONAL VERSION® and NIV® are
registered trademarks of Biblica, Inc. Use of either trademark for the offering
of goods or services requires the prior written consent of Biblica US, Inc.

This book is a work of non-fiction. Unless otherwise noted, the author
and the publisher make no explicit guarantees as to the accuracy of
the information contained in this book and in some cases, names of
people and places have been altered to protect their privacy.

WestBow Press books may be ordered through booksellers or by contacting:

WestBow Press
A Division of Thomas Nelson & Zondervan
1663 Liberty Drive
Bloomington, IN 47403
www.westbowpress.com
1 (866) 928-1240

Because of the dynamic nature of the Internet, any web addresses or
links contained in this book may have changed since publication and
may no longer be valid. The views expressed in this work are solely those
of the author and do not necessarily reflect the views of the publisher,
and the publisher hereby disclaims any responsibility for them.

Any people depicted in stock imagery provided by Thinkstock are models,
and such images are being used for illustrative purposes only.
Certain stock imagery © Thinkstock.

ISBN: 978-1-5127-6297-6 (sc)
ISBN: 978-1-5127-6299-0 (hc)
ISBN: 978-1-5127-6298-3 (e)

Library of Congress Control Number: 2016918486

Print information available on the last page.

WestBow Press rev. date: 11/14/2016

To Libba, who showed me a brighter light.

CONTENTS

INTRODUCTION

Brace yourself like a man; I will question
you, and you shall answer me.
—Job 40:7

The Method of Questions

In his book, *The Bible Jesus Read*, Philip Yancey relates
seeing graffiti stating that "Jesus is the answer." Over
this, someone had scrawled, "So what's the question?"
The author goes on to express and discuss some
questions he sees posited in the Bible that Jesus read:
the Hebrew scriptures.[1] Since my earliest readings
of scripture, I have been struck by how many times
God poses questions to his people. We go to the

---

[1] Yancey, Philip. *The Bible Jesus Read*, Zondervan
Publishing House, 1999.

Bible seeking the answers to our deepest questions about life, community, and death. And, so often, what we find are questions from God.

A common method of encouraging people to think through important issues and to learn important truths is the method of asking questions. Like the statement to Job above, the questions that God asks His people are asked because *we* need to know the answers. If we were simply presented with the answers as a set of stated facts, we would not grasp their true meaning and purpose. We would not make these facts truly a part of our worldview. And, thus, we could not be fully guided by these truths.

Perhaps one of the most famous teachers to use this method was Socrates. Socrates spent much of his time wandering the streets of ancient Athens, engaging people he met in conversation. But his conversations were a means of learning and teaching. He would pose a question to whoever would engage him. The response would invariably lead to more questions. In this way, people would be led to discover truths about themselves and their world that they had already known but had never taken the time to explore in an orderly and contemplative way. The Socratic method of questioning ideas in an orderly and logical fashion makes use of one's ability to reason coupled with one's experiences to gain a deeper understanding of oneself and the world.

It has been said that the best teacher is experience. Truly, the best teacher is someone else's experience that we can observe and from which we can learn without having to experience the associated tribulations. But people usually have to relive these instances themselves rather than learn from other people's experiences. Thus, the root of the saying that those ignorant of history are doomed to repeat it.

I am very impressed with the scientific method as a means of gaining understanding. The progress attained in the various realms of science and engineering attest to the power of this method. Of course, when dealing with history, one cannot easily conduct repeatable experiments. But the root of the scientific method is careful and well-documented observations coupled with hypothesized interpretations. Continual observations and attempts to learn from these observations enhance our understanding of fundamental underlying truths.

The Bible is generally a recording of other people's experiences. The supposition is that we can learn from studying these events. However, care must be taken to understand the relating of the experience and the observer's attempt at an interpretation. This is especially true of the Old Testament. I believe there are many instances where events are interpreted based on the limited understanding of the times. We should always be careful to distinguish the reporting of an experience from the editorial comments of the observer. And we should examine the interpretation based on the entire scripture together with our own life experiences and the use of our reasoning.

Many of the experiences related in the scriptures include one or more questions from God to his people. God surely knows the answer and poses these questions for our benefit. At times it helps to rephrase the question to see the true meaning of the question posed. I hope in this brief note to assist the reader in the exploration of just a few of the many questions raised by God in the scriptures. I hope this study encourages you to find more questions and to continue to seek the answers.

Small Group Study

I have tried to make this book useful as an individual read. But my hope is that you use this book as a guide and stimulus for a six-week small group study. In the manner of Socrates, John Wesley, and others, I believe that a useful assist to learning is to say your questions and answers aloud and to hear how they sound when spoken to others.

Also, you will be able to better clarify your thoughts by hearing how others respond to these same questions. I am mindful of the description of people given in Genesis 2:18: "It is not good for the man to be alone." And, as you explore these questions, you will form a bond to the small group of persons with whom you share this study. Hopefully, that bond continues and grows beyond this study.

Let me suggest a *small group study format.* Choose a facilitator. This person will not have the answers any more than anyone else in the group. But this person should take the time to read over the material prior to the group meeting to gain some familiarity with the topic. The facilitator should seek to keep the conversation flowing, with care not to dominate the discussion.

The group can decide to have the same facilitator each session, but I recommend that the group have a different facilitator for each session. In this way, the perspectives of each member can be better shared. And this gives everyone the experience of posing faith questions to others.

In each of the chapters, a question is posed together with a main Old Testament reference. The question, as well as its surrounding context from the scriptures, should be read aloud at the beginning of the session if it has not been read prior to the meeting. The text in this book provides a brief description of the scripture story as witnessed and presented in the Bible. At this point, the group should discuss the scripture scene and the main question. Think through and discuss the events and the context for this question.

Next, the text identifies related questions with one or more additional Old Testament scripture references. These too should be read aloud. Important questions are never asked just one time. The text contains some further discussion of the questions and the scriptures, and how all of these relate to the fundamental question posed for the session. If time is a constraint, the facilitator may select from the several Old Testament scriptures suggested depending on the flow of the discussion.

I believe the answer is in these Old Testament scriptures. But, as the title suggests, the answer should also be found in the New Testament. After the group has wrestled with the question and come to some understanding, the text provides New

Testament references where it is suggested that scripture provides clarification to these questions and answers. These references can be introduced and read aloud to stimulate more discussion.

Finally, each chapter ends with a brief session outline with several suggestions to stimulate the discussion.

Additional Thoughts

God would not ask a question knowing you could not find the answer. Jesus asserts that He is the answer. And He asserts that the Old Testament is describing Him so that He would be known by others when He came (John 5:39–40). So I encourage you to join with others to explore these questions. But do so freely, with the understanding that God *wants* these questions explored. Exercise is meant to change your external aspect and feed your physical health. Information is meant to change your inner formation and feed your spiritual health.

God does not leave us in a void with no guidance. It

is important to see the group discussion as a dialogue with God. He wants us to understand. But He wants us to seek the answers in such a way that we attain a deeper understanding than if we were given a set of tenets to memorize. These questions are intended to lead to an understanding and clarification of our worldview that is truly a part of our being.

Again, the answers to these questions are in the scriptures and in you. However, the details and emphasis of the answers will change with your life experience and life events. Your answer today may have changed somewhat from your answer years ago. And you may question the validity of your response to these questions. Do not be afraid to express doubts. It was the doubt of Thomas that led to a deeper understanding and faith when Jesus presented him with more information.

I have deliberately kept the text in this book to a minimum. My goal is to point you to the scripture texts in your Bible. While I briefly describe the scripture verses, I assume the readers will precede each section by reading the scripture reference. In the group, it is common for several individuals to have different Bible translations. This may lead to more discussion than otherwise as you review subtleties in scripture translations.

I assume God asks these questions because they are important. God wants us to think about our responses. Certainly, God knows the answers. He asks us to think about these questions for our benefit and for our enrichment. And so I invite you to join in a dialogue with God and to go with others on a journey to a deeper understanding of your Lord.

CHAPTER 1

WHO IS YOUR LORD?

Where are you?
—Genesis 3:9

Who told you, that you were naked?
—Genesis 3:11

Scripture Reading: Genesis 2:25–3:24

The Bible Question

At the end of Genesis 2 (the second creation story), man and woman were living together in the garden of Eden, in paradise. God had placed them there, and He had given them all they needed to reside together in joy and contentment. He had also given

1

them the responsibility to care for the land and all of its inhabitants.

They had been told that they were free to eat from any tree in the garden, except for the fruit from the Tree of Knowledge. And it became clear that God planned to commune with them during His walks in this garden. He planned to have daily worship. This is worship as it was meant to be with God and people relating as family and friends.

In the ancient Middle East, the lord and supreme ruler often had a garden adjoined to his palatial residence. This garden was cared for by his stewards. Periodically, the lord would walk through his garden for relaxation and contemplation. It was seen as an extreme honor to be allowed to commune with the lord on these walks. Everyone knew who owned the garden. And one felt honored to be asked to share the garden with the owner.

Day after day, Adam and Eve cared for the garden of Eden and its animals. And every day, they communed with God in a worship time. Thus, the picture in Genesis is one of joy, contentment, peace, and extreme privilege.

Genesis 3 opens with the serpent posing questions that begin, "Did God really say …" It seems the serpent counted on Eve not truly knowing God and His motivation. These questions seem designed to challenge the authority of God. I believe what was being asked is, "Is your God trustworthy?" and "Do you trust God to set the rules?" Eve was engaged in a dialogue about what God said, what God really meant, and, of course, why God should be the rule-maker.

The serpent suggested answers to the questions he posed. "God is a jealous God, and He has His own interests, not yours, as the motivation for His commands." While God had made Adam and Eve rulers over the garden for their benefit, the serpent claimed that God's motivation was selfishness. The serpent described a jealous God who was not being truthful rather than the God who had freely given privilege and authority. The serpent maintained that

3

the real truth was "you will be like God, knowing good and evil." I believe he convinced Eve she could earn this status through her own efforts by merely disobeying God and eating from the Tree of Knowledge of Good and Evil.

God told them not to eat of the Tree of Knowledge or they would die. The serpent seemed to say the world could be as they imagined or desired; they could create it in their image. Somehow this tree contained a powerful magic that would change the order of the world.

Adam and Eve became victims to thinking that the world could be made as they imagined rather than relying on their observations of how the world actually was. Do we believe with reason and experience or do we stubbornly hold to our preconceived notions? And, after all, what does it mean that they would die? They would learn that this death was willful separation from God.

After Eve and Adam ate from the Tree of Knowledge, they realized they had disappointed God, and what they learned from their actions was shame and fear. They saw their worth as much diminished from how they saw it when in the presence of God. Before, when they gazed on the glory of God, they saw themselves as God saw them. He saw them as children, royalty, and treasures to be nurtured. Their focus was on the Lord.

Now their focus was on themselves. Now they saw themselves in the eyes of the serpent—not as stewards, but as destroyers. Not as treasures, but as guilt-ridden, disobedient animals.

With this knowledge, they saw themselves as unworthy of the trust God had granted them. They deserved judgment. They had willfully separated themselves from God; they judged themselves unworthy. And so, Adam and Eve attempted to correct the situation by making garments of fig leaves for themselves. But they still felt shame and realized their efforts fell short of their purpose.

God knows His children. He knows what they have done. He knows where they are. And yet He calls out with the question, "Where are you?" I believe He wanted them to recognize, acknowledge, and know God.

Adam, coming out from the bushes, explained his shame and fear. He admitted his sin, but he did not recognize the God of mercy. Adam saw a reflection of himself; he saw a God of judgment. Man had changed the relationship, not God.

God asked, "Who told you that you were naked?" To my understanding, God seemed to be asking, "Have you sinned? Have you disobeyed Me? Do you know Me, the God of love?" And rather than admitting to his Father his disobedience, Adam tried to explain what had happened and why. And he tried to explain why it was not really his fault. God made the world (and Eve), so it must be God's fault. Adam became legalistic. He began to rank and judge everything and everyone.

Take some time to think about this scene. What do you think God is really asking of His creation? When He asks, "Where are you?" isn't He asking where you are in your faith? When God says, "Who told you, you are naked?" is He perhaps asking to whom you really listen when seeking the truth?

We, like Adam and Eve, judge the sin for God. And so we fear God. Thinking of what you know of the character of Jesus, would God have forgiven Adam and Eve if they had just admitted their disobedience and repented?

The Question Again

Rather than admit his shame, Adam reacts with a false pride. Just as the many prophets have warned, Ezekiel 28:1–10 speaks of man's pride. These are harsh words to hear.

Have you ever felt too proud? Or have you ever tried to convince yourself that you are not getting what you believe you deserve? Have you ever felt the despair of the realization that you have been too proud?

Read Deuteronomy 31:14–29. Just as God knew that the Israelites would become proud, God always knew what Adam and Eve had done. In Deuteronomy 32, Moses relates how God is faithful and just. It is a picture of God that Adam and Eve assumed. But this is a picture of God that reflects humanity's limited understanding of law and justice. It shows a lack of understanding of God's love and mercy for His children. It shows a lack of understanding of God's grace.

When God comes to commune with His children, as was the custom, God comes for their daily worship time. Worship should be communication. And yet they hid because they feared that God would see them as they now saw themselves. They no longer feared God with reverential awe, but rather they feared God with dread. They had assumed a new view of themselves, and they did not have a true understanding of God.

While Adam and Eve knew of good and evil, they did not yet know of mercy and grace. Mercy is at the Tree of Life. God never said they could not eat of the Tree of Life. But now He built a hedge around it until He could teach His children to truly know and trust their Lord.

The Lord wants His people to understand that, as hopeless as things look to us, God is the source of life. Adam and Eve believed that all was lost; they would surely die. But they did not understand or remember the Tree of Life.

God asked Ezekiel to look upon a field of dry bones (Ezekiel 37:1–14). He saw a field of barren desolation. Looking at the field of dry bones, God asked Ezekiel if these bones could live. Surely they could not. But unlike Adam, Ezekiel gave the correct answer: "O Sovereign Lord, You alone know."

Knowing this time in the history of the Hebrews is important to understanding the true meaning of this scene. These people had their many stories in Genesis, stories of Noah, Abraham, Isaac, Jacob, and then Moses. They knew of the promises of God and His mighty acts on their behalf.

In 1 and 2 Samuel, there are the stories of the

fulfillment of these promises as they understood them with the creation of a safe and united kingdom under David and then under Solomon. They believed they were secure with their God, His temple, and the ark.

But now the Babylonians had sacked Jerusalem, destroyed the temple, and taken many people as captives across hundreds of miles of desert. As they tried with utter hopelessness to grasp the situation and what it meant, Ezekiel related this experience he had with God.

God slowly led Ezekiel to a deeper understanding of their relationship and their situation. When Ezekiel obeyed God and prophesied to the bones, he saw the dry bones come together. At the obedient words of Ezekiel, the bones came together and were covered with flesh and skin. However, they were still without life. God instructed Ezekiel to command the breath of life to enter the risen bones. With Ezekiel's obedience came renewed life and a deeper understanding.

God's instructions to Ezekiel serve several purposes.

First, when there seems to be no hope, God can still work through His people. And God will not abandon His people in their time of need. Hopelessness is not in the vocabulary of God or God's children.

Examine these verses as God demonstrates how, with the Lord to guide him, Ezekiel could see these dry bones live. Again, we focus on the obvious— justice—while God focuses on life and grace.

A Bible Answer–The God of Love and Grace

The best way to learn about someone is through extended and close interaction. It is necessary to see the person react to positive and negative circumstances. It is necessary to hear them express their views on many subjects and situations. You cannot know someone's true character by focusing on a single event.

Many people focus on the power of God demonstrated by the major events in the Old Testament, like parting the Red Sea and destroying Sodom and Gomorrah, but they ignore the grace and mercy. Many people focus on the kindness and miracles of Jesus described in the New Testament and ignore His harsh requirements and judgments. Obviously, we must learn a full and balanced description of the character of God.

The Bible presents a view of God through the lens of many people and many experiences. We use the scriptures to view these experiences of others for our edification. Sometimes we accept literally the conclusions about God drawn by these ancient observers. Be careful to distinguish the experience from the observer's interpretation. We must use these many experiences together with our own experiences and our reason to perceive the true character of God.

The point of this chapter and God's questioning is twofold. First, one needs to discern the nature of God: to learn His character, to understand His motivation. Most of all, you need to truly know who it is that you decide to follow and obey (Luke

14: 25–33). Second, you must make a conscious decision as to what is your focus and motivation. In exchange for our commitment, God offers an intimate relationship. Nowhere does the Bible say this world has no suffering. But when troubles and sufferings occur, God promises a peace and assurance that comes with this commitment and understanding.

In His many interactions with sinners, Jesus clearly expressed mercy and compassion. He would always admonish the sinner to "sin no more," but this was always expressed with grace. Jesus knows that we can live to the standard He set and demonstrated. He fully expects people can act with compassion and mercy to others. Jesus demonstrated this characteristic of God during His life (John 14:12).

Adam and Eve did not understand or realize this aspect of the character of God. They used their human understanding to focus on what was just and fair in their own eyes. They assumed God would respond to them in this manner.

The disciples lived with Jesus for several years. They watched and listened as He interacted with many people and in many situations. He told them that when they saw Him, they saw the Father (John 14:1–14). And He asked them, "Who do you say I am?" (Luke 9:18–27). As with the transfiguration episode, Jesus is demonstrating the subtle difference between what His people have learned from their patriarchs and prophets versus what they are learning from His example. If we keep our focus on God, we too can behave in accordance with the kingdom of heaven. He is the example.

Small Group Outline

Discuss: Who is your Lord?

Scripture Reading: Genesis 2:25 through 3:24

What is God really asking His children in this exchange? When God asks, "Where are you?" is He perhaps asking where you are in your understanding of God?

On many occasions, God says, "Fear not!" When God says, "Who told you, you are naked?" is He perhaps asking you to examine the source of your fear? Why are you hiding from God? Can you hide from God?

Notes:

Scripture Reading: Deuteronomy chapter 32; Ezekiel 37:1–14

What do these verses say about human pride?

What do these verses say about justice and grace?

How does the dialogue with Ezekiel give hope at a time of seeming hopelessness?

Relate the situation of Ezekiel and the Hebrews to the situation of the disciples after the crucifixion but before the resurrection.

Notes:

Scripture Reading: John 14:1–14, Luke 9:18–27, Luke 14:25–33

Compare the character of God displayed in the Old Testament with that of the New Testament. Remember that Jesus claimed They were one and the same.

Thinking of what you know of the character of Jesus, would God have forgiven Adam and Eve if they had just admitted their disobedience and repented?

Consider the cost of what Jesus asks of His followers.

Notes:

CHAPTER 2

WHO ARE YOU?

What is your name?

—Genesis 32:27

Scripture reading: Genesis 25:19 through 33:20

The Bible Question

The subject question is toward the end of a long and detailed account of the patriarch, Jacob, one of the sons of Isaac. Isaac and Rebekah had twin sons. The first born (the oldest) was Esau, and the younger twin was Jacob. Now Esau was a real man's man. Esau made his dad proud. Esau worked in the open, hunting wild beasts and managing the domestic animals. Jacob, on the other hand, was a mama's boy. Jacob learned to cook and sew as he hung out with the women, probably doing many other girlie chores.

There are a few things that I am sure Jacob heard many times while growing up as a small boy. Jacob's grandfather, Abraham, had an older son, Ishmael, and then a second son, Isaac. Isaac learned from Abraham, and I'm sure taught his sons the legal importance of getting the blessing of the father. The oldest son was the heir of the double share of his father's estate. He had this through his birthright. But the real key was to have the father specifically state their inheritances. This was done by the father giving his sons his blessing. This had to be especially important to Isaac because he was the younger of Abraham's first two sons.

Jacob knew well the story of Ishmael and Isaac. He knew the importance and meaning of birthrights and blessings from the father. He knew about Ishmael being sent away to die. *He also knew the personal pain of watching his father obviously favor Esau. This had to hurt him.*

Now besides being a mama's boy, Jacob inherited his mother's trait of being sneaky and conspiring. When he was a young lad, Jacob tricked Esau into selling his birthright for a bowl of stew. For this, Esau despised Jacob. Jacob didn't seem to care how Esau was hurt. Later, Rebekah instructed Jacob on how to trick the very elderly Isaac into giving his full blessing to Jacob, all the while thinking he was giving this blessing to Esau. This time Esau swore to kill Jacob. Again, Jacob did not seem to care how Esau was hurt, but he took seriously the threat to kill him.

And so, Jacob ran from Esau, fleeing to his uncle, Laban. Soon after Jacob arrived, he wanted to marry Rachel, the beautiful younger daughter of Laban. So Jacob and Laban made an agreement. Jacob was to work for Laban for seven years, tending his flocks. After the seven years, Jacob would marry Rachel. Ah, the romance!

Day after day, Jacob had to do the man's work he so despised to gain his prize. And after years of toil, he achieved his goal. But it turns out that Laban was every bit as tricky as his sister and Jacob. After the wedding feast, Laban switched daughters, and Jacob wound up with Leah, the older daughter.

Jacob immediately protested that he wanted to marry Rachel, not Leah. (Side note, especially ladies in the group: How would you feel if your groom went to your dad on the day after your wedding night and said, "I didn't want to marry her. I wanted the pretty sister.") Laban modified the agreement, and Jacob agreed to toil many more years for a second bride.

Being alone and working hard for many years provided much opportunity for introspection. As Jacob toiled, I suspect he had plenty of time to think about how he had treated others—how he had tricked Esau and stole what was rightly his. For years, Jacob watched the reaction of Leah and Rachel to his words and actions as they bickered and fussed with each other. Maybe, finally, Jacob (knowing how

21

he was hurt by his father's favoritism) knew how he had hurt Leah, and how so long ago he had hurt his brother, Esau. Did he finally feel their pain? Did Jacob truly see himself with shame, like Adam and Eve in the garden?

While having achieved wives, children, servants, and wealth, Jacob had finally learned empathy. Jacob needed to let Esau know he deeply regretted his previous behavior. And so, he returned to face Esau. He returned humbled, finally seeing himself as others saw him: as Jacob the swindler. He returned expecting Esau might seek revenge and kill him. That was what he justly deserved. But he risked everything to no longer be that Jacob.

As he fearfully approached his brother, it says Jacob wrestled with God. What does this scene really mean? Was God trying to get Jacob to dig deep into his soul to better understand himself and his motivations? Was he still Jacob the schemer and cheat? Was he trying to appease Esau and justify his prior actions?

Or was he now Jacob, the father of God's people, filled with empathy?

I believe Jacob had to decide if he was sincere in wanting Esau to have what he deserved. So, as they wrestled, God would not let him go until Jacob saw himself the way God always saw him: not as Jacob the swindler, but as Israel, the one who carried the promise of God. After much anguish, capping his years of toil and introspection, God asked Jacob, "What is your name?" Knowing the importance of names and their meaning in Hebrew scriptures, I believe God was asking Jacob, "How do you see yourself?"

And he answered, "I am Jacob."

God corrected him, saying, "Your name will no longer be Jacob, but Israel, because you have struggled with God and with men and have overcome." I believe God was telling him that He had always seen him as Israel, an example to His people.

Israel would always remember the old Jacob, as

evidenced by his limp, but he would never again be that Jacob; he would now be the person God knew as Israel. From then on, when he interacted with others, he would do so with compassion and empathy. Having learned from his experiences, he could feel the pain of his hurtful actions to others, and he could feel the joy of his kindnesses to others. *Israel was not Jacob because he would always remember Jacob. He was Israel because God saw him as Israel. And he trusted God.*

The Question Again

Many years later, when God brought the Israelites out of Egypt, He gave Moses many rules and laws. Many of these were guidelines on how to provide support for the poor and the less fortunate in their times of need. These laws are detailed in Deuteronomy and other early books of the Bible. For example, in Deuteronomy 5:15 is the command to keep the Sabbath day as a day to worship the Lord and rest. But it's not enough to stop working yourself. You must not make your servants work either. Don't even make your animals work. And don't make the aliens who are among you work, whether they worship the Lord or not. Why act this way? Not because it is a law, but "Remember you were slaves in Egypt." You know what it is like to long for rest.

In Deuteronomy 15:1–11, God's law says that every seventh year, all debts will be cancelled. God even said not to think in the sixth year that you had better not loan that person in trouble any money, because next year the debt will get cancelled, and you will not get paid back. You are to go ahead and be generous to that person who needs help. In the Sabbath year, all indentured servants were to be set free (Deuteronomy 15:12–18). And, God said to not send them away empty-handed; supply them liberally with sheep and grain and wine. Why act this way? "Remember that you were slaves in Egypt and the Lord your God redeemed you. That is why I give you this command today." (Deuteronomy 15:15)

Deuteronomy 24:17–18 is about justice and generosity.

"Do not deprive the alien or the fatherless of justice, or take the cloak of the widow as a pledge." It is all she has to keep her warm. Just lend the money to her freely. Why? "Remember that you were slaves in Egypt."

Deuteronomy 24:19–22 is about gleaning. This law says that if you miss part of your crop when you are harvesting, do not go back over the field a second time. Leave the leftovers for the aliens, the orphans, and the widows. Why? "Remember that you were slaves in Egypt." Remember that you were poor; you were powerless and oppressed. And let that memory shape the way you act when you are free. So remembering and empathy function as the basis for ethics in the Old Testament.

The key for our discussion is that *we should know the right thing to do by relating to our life experiences and our Bible studies.* Don't hold on to bitterness for the sake of vengeance, but rather remember how you felt so you will know how to act with compassion, empathy, mercy, and understanding. Having laws will not compel proper behavior. Having the love of God and understanding how the other person would want to be treated will give you the capacity to know proper behavior.

Consider a favorite Bible story: Job. At the beginning of this book, it is related that Job is a righteous man who shares his wealth with the less fortunate members of his community. I am sure he was sincere in his caring. But then Job loses everything: his children all die, his wealth is lost, and then finally his health is gone. He is covered with sores and living in total poverty. He is helpless and totally dependent.

Much of the text of this book is Job and a few friends trying to interpret this situation. At the end, miraculously, Job regains even greater wealth than before. Once again, he is generous to the less fortunate. *But how does he see the poor now?* I am sure that before he was sincere. But now, when he sees these less fortunate people, he can relate more sincerely because he remembers and can relate to when he was destitute.

The whole of the God's Law is based on treating others as you would want to be treated: empathy. Read 2 Samuel 11. Then read in 2 Samuel 12:1–10 as Nathan helps King David to see how he is acting toward others through a simple parable.

A Bible Answer: Seeing All People as Children of God

The Bible is useful in many different ways, but two of its main uses are as a guide on how we are to relate to God and how we are to relate to one another. These are summarized nicely in the question and answer given in Luke 10:25–37.

Jesus was questioned by an expert in the Law on what he must do to inherit eternal life. They agree that to inherit eternal life, the Law commands, "To love God, and to love your neighbor as yourself." (Leviticus 19:18) However, this expert needs clarification on the exact definition of the word *neighbor*. He obviously doesn't want to waste his love on those who are not legally defined as his neighbors.

And so Jesus relates the parable of the Good Samaritan. In this parable, a traveler has been mugged, robbed, beaten, and left to die by the side of the road. He obviously needs help. The priest and the Levite cross to the other side of the road to avoid him. The Samaritan stops, cleans the man's wounds, and secures him shelter and care; he sacrifices his time and possessions to assist the stranger with no expectation of reward. He had genuine mercy and compassion on this traveler.

When speaking about this parable, Dr. Martin Luther King, Jr. stated[2], "The first question which the priest and the Levite asked was: 'If I stop to help this man, what will happen to me?' But the Samaritan reversed the question: 'If I don't stop to help this man, what will happen to him?'" So I think we need to go beyond the ever popular, "What would Jesus do?" Empathy is how we can *know* what to do.

Thus, when we are commanded to "Love your

---

[2] Edited by James Washington, *Martin Luther King, Jr., I Have A Dream.* Harper San Francisco, 1992.

neighbor as you love yourself," we are being commanded to empathize. We are being commanded to remember our life experiences and Bible lessons for the purpose of trying to understand *how each of us would want to be treated* in this situation. Remember to always edify others and not tear down; remember to care; remember to put others first; remember to be a servant to all people and to not be self-serving. Remember to have compassion, have mercy, and view yourself on the receiving side of your actions. Remember when you were Jacob so that you can always be Israel.

So our guide in treating others is our empathy: the ability to see how we would want to be treated. And we can learn from our mistakes and shortcomings. But we must not continually denigrate ourselves. We should humbly and honestly see ourselves in truth. And yet, we need to realize that God sees our potential when He says we are His friends, brothers, and heirs to the kingdom. God sees us truthfully, but He also sees us as He intends us to be. He sees who we can be.

Small Group Outline

Discuss: Who are you?

Scripture Reading: Genesis 25:19 through 33:20

Discuss how Jacob learned to sense the impact of his words and actions on others.

Review times when someone has hurt your feelings without even being aware of the impact on you.

Discuss how children must learn to understand the impact of their words and actions on those around them.

Notes:

Scripture Reading: Deuteronomy 5:15; 15:1–18; 24:17–22

Discuss a guide for community life based on empathy rather than rules and punishments. How are the commands in the Jewish Law based on empathy?

How would world politics change if nations acted based on empathy?

Scripture Reading: 2 Samuel 11 and 12:1–10

How did Nathan use this parable to help David understand how his actions had hurt others?

Think about how you see yourself when speaking or acting.

Now try to imagine how others may react to your words and actions.

Notes:

Scripture Reading: Luke 10:25–37.

Discuss how Jesus quoted the Golden Rule from the Old Testament as a way to summarize not just the commands of the Law, but also the intent of the Law or a moral compass.

Consider our Declaration of Independence as a moral compass and our Constitution as the commands of Law.

Reflect on the specific events from the life of Jesus where He demonstrated empathy.

Reflect on spiritual leaders, such as Reverend Martin Luther King Jr., Mahatma Gandhi, Nelson Mandela, and Reverend Billy Graham. How did empathy guide their lives?

How does the way we see ourselves impact our lives?

Discuss the question of who we are as evidenced not by to what group we belong, but rather as evidenced by what we do and say.

Notes:

CHAPTER 3

WHAT DO YOU NEED?

What is that in your hand?
—Exodus 4:2

Scripture Reading: Exodus chapters 2 through 4

The Bible Question

When Jacob's family arrived in Egypt, Joseph had already provided a great service to the Egyptians. By the book of Exodus, the Israelites had been in Egypt some four hundred years. While at first they were welcomed, by the time of this scripture, they were subjugated and made to work as slaves. The

Egyptians doubted their loyalty and, so, feared the many Hebrews in their midst.

The Israelite Moses was born into this society and given the option of living as Egyptian nobility rather than as an Israelite slave. But Moses had compassion for his people. After watching the ill treatment of some Israelites by an Egyptian, Moses sought justice by slaying the Egyptian. Neither the Israelites nor the Egyptians took this action well. And so Moses fled. While Moses felt empathy for the Israelites, his attempt to bring them justice met with failure.

Exodus chapter 3 begins with Moses serving as a shepherd for his father-in-law. While he tended the sheep, he saw a bush aglow with fire, but not being consumed. Curious, Moses approached to get a closer look. Now God had his attention and spoke. First, He let Moses know that He was the God of His people. And He told Moses that just as Moses felt the pain of these people, so did their God. Thus, God had come to free His people. But the message from God was that He was sending Moses to lead His people to freedom.

Moses previously sought to free the Israelites by exacting justice. Now God told Moses to command Pharaoh to free the Israelites with mercy. In response, Moses asked the wrong question. He asked, "Who am I that I should go to Pharaoh and bring the Israelites out of Egypt?" It does not matter who you are. The correct question is "What do you need?" And so God gave the answer to the correct question: "I will be with you."

Continuing, Moses again said the Israelites and the Egyptians would not listen to him. Moses did not see that he had any way of convincing the others of the presence of God. But the lesson Moses had to learn was that whatever he had or whoever he was, what was important was that God was with him. And so when Moses said he did not have the skills necessary and that the others would not believe him, God asked Moses to examine what he already had. In Chapter 4 verse 2, God asked Moses to examine himself: "What is that in your hand?" You see, whatever assets Moses already possessed could be used to accomplish this mission *as long as God was with him*. At this point, God showed Moses through the conversion of his staff into a snake and back, and through other miracles, that He would be with Moses.

At the end of chapter 4, Moses witnessed to Aaron. Then Aaron witnessed to the elders. In this way, all of the Israelites learned that God cared for them, and so they worshiped God. They were still slaves in Egypt. Yet they worshiped God because He cared. He cared, and He was with them in their suffering.

The people had their Genesis tales about God and about their patriarchs. They knew of Jacob and how he had been shown empathy. Moses knew these things. He had attempted to gain justice for the people on his own only to be rebuffed by both the Israelites and the Egyptians. What Moses was lacking was for God to be with him and for him to witness to others about the mercy of God. Whatever else Moses needed was whatever he already had.

Think about the stories of the Old Testament. Think about how God uses people to accomplish acts of mercy and justice. While we want fire and brimstone, God asks people to act with kindness and understanding. Reflect on times when you had to accomplish seemingly impossible tasks with few resources.

In the last session, we explored the need to understand who we are through an honest look at ourselves, and to view ourselves as God sees us. Now we are being asked to consider the resources available to us instead of focusing on what we lack. When God gave Moses his mission, Moses constantly looked to what he lacked. God kept coming back to the fact that He would be with Moses.

The Question Again

Examine the story of Gideon in Judges chapters 6 and

7. The life of the Israelites at this time was miserable. They were hiding in caves, and their enemies were spoiling their means of survival at every opportunity. They were praying for God to save them. But their prophets told them that God was angered because they had willfully worshiped other Gods when He returned them to the Promised Land. Thus, they accepted their fate and wallowed in their misery.

And so, as Gideon secretly and timidly worked at feeding his family, he was greeted by an angel who said, "The Lord is with you, mighty warrior." Gideon's response was the same as ours would be and often is. We look at our circumstances and see what we lack. We focus on the hardship. We would try harder if we only had more. We could do more if only we were given more. Gideon's response was to question how God could be with them if all these bad things were happening.

God's response was, "Go in the strength you have and save Israel ... Am I not sending you?" This is God's response to our focus on the hard circumstances and what we lack: "Am I not sending you?" Remember—He told Moses, "I am with you. Use whatever you have; I have given you enough."

And so God sent a message to Gideon that the Lord was with him. Gideon did not see himself as a mighty warrior. And he doubted that the Lord was with him because he saw no evidence of this. Just like Moses, Gideon doubted the word of God because he saw himself as destitute and lacking—not as God saw him. But the command was given: go in the strength you have and save Israel.

Again Gideon looked at himself and his kinsmen. *How can I save Israel when I am weak?* So God commanded Gideon to destroy the altar that his father erected to Baal. The Lord comes before obedience to family and friends. Gideon did as commanded, but he did it at night because he was afraid. As Gideon accomplished these smaller tasks, he gained confidence in himself and in his God.

I particularly like Judges chapter 7. Gideon gathered a fighting force of thirty-two thousand men. God told Gideon not to depend on all of these men, but to trust God. And so many were sent away, and then there were ten thousand men. Next God told him that all he needed was to know God was with him. And so Gideon sent away more until there were only three hundred men left. In this way, the people would know it was not by their strength that they won the day. Gideon was hailed as God's mighty warrior before he had ever fought a battle or led an army. Next he was shown that he could either have thousands of men with him, or he could rely on God's promises.

A Bible Answer: The Joy of Assurance

In John 2:1–11, Jesus, his mother, and some disciples were attending a wedding party. We are not told much more about this event or the families of the newly married couple. During the party, the host ran out of wine. This would be a social embarrassment for the families, but seemingly no obvious great event in the plans of God. Mary brought this to the attention of her son. His response was, "Dear woman, why do you involve me?" (Mary's reply was not recorded. I can imagine her response was simply that look one gets from his mother when she expects more of her son at a social function, such as a church potluck dinner.)

But consider the reply of Jesus in light of the questions of Moses when he sought justice for the Israelites in Egypt so many centuries before. Moses had acted with good intentions. Moses sought justice for the Israelites. But he had acted alone. Why not involve God? When he later returned, God was with him. God was with him, and God instructed him to expect mercy and grace.

When Gideon was alone, he trembled before his enemies. Should Gideon not have involved God? When we go it alone, we go with fear and trepidation. When we involve God, He gives His assurance, His peace, and His joy. Whenever we face hard times or good times, why not involve God? What else do we need?

43

In the Gospel of John, several of the disciples were seeking someone who could give them hope. At the urging of John, they followed Jesus. He turned to ask, "What do you want?" (John 1:35–39). And, finally, when the disciples were utterly devastated and facing hopelessness after the death of Jesus, He greeted the women at the tomb with the questions, "Woman, why are you crying? Who is it you are looking for?" (John 20:1–18).

God is still seeking for us to realize what and who we need.

Small Group Outline

Discuss: What do you need?

Scripture Reading: Exodus chapters 2 through 4

Discuss the difference in seeking justice and seeking mercy.

Discuss the effect of a focus on what you lack versus a focus on what you have.

Reflect on your particular talents and personal resources to be a witness to and to serve others.

Have the group reflect on what talents they see in other group members.

Notes:

Scripture Reading: Judges chapters 6 and 7

Consider the experiences described in the scriptures and how these people persevered with their God-given talents and the assurance that God was with them.

When have you hesitated to act because you lacked the required resources?

Read and discuss the contentment and joy of Paul (Philippians 4:12–13).

Notes:

Scripture Reading: John 2:1–11; John 1:35–39; John 20:1–18

Describe a time when you faced a circumstance or event with fear and trepidation.

Describe how the presence of God gives assurance, peace, and joy.

Discuss the need to involve God when we face both hard times and good times.

Notes:

CHAPTER 4

DO YOU UNDERSTAND?

Have I not commanded you?
—Joshua 1:9

Scripture Reading: Joshua 1 through 6:25

The Bible Question

In the early chapters of the book of Joshua, there were several encounters between Joshua and the Lord. In the first encounter (Joshua 1:1–9) the Lord stated clearly to Joshua that now that Moses was not there to lead the Israelites, it was up to Joshua to lead them. But the main message was that just as the Lord was with Moses, so He was now with Joshua.

Joshua was commanded to be strong and courageous before the Lord's people in representing God. Joshua was commanded to listen and obey. He was instructed to remember all he had learned while at the side of Moses. He was commanded to keep the scriptures close at hand. In the midst of the instructions was the question for Joshua to contemplate: "Have I not commanded you?" I believe that perhaps God was asking, "Do you understand what I am telling you?"

Joshua immediately told his officers to prepare to cross into the Promised Land. As part of the preparations, Joshua sent spies to investigate the situation in Jericho. This was not to doubt the Lord. Rather this was in keeping with the commands to count the cost of obeying before committing (See the parable of Jesus in Luke 14).

Plus (as with much of the Old Testament) taking Jericho was to be a shadow of God's full plan to bring His people back into relationship. From Rahab, the spies learned the condition of the defenses in Jericho. And they learned of the low morale in Jericho. Most important, they learned of a means of entry and exit through the inn under the protection of Rahab.

The spies promised that the family of Rahab could gain salvation by making an outward sign of obedience to God. The sign was a red signal on the entryway to attest that all of the occupants were people loyal to God. This was exactly what was commanded previously at the Passover in Egypt. The blood of the lamb on the doorpost was an outward symbol of their trust in God.

In Joshua chapter 3, the people made final preparations to cross the Jordan. They trusted that the Lord was with the army and with Joshua, but they did not have a personal relationship yet. They would follow the ark, but at a distance. Once again, the Lord parted the sea to allow His people to cross the water.

As they approached Jericho, Joshua saw a man with a sword in his hand blocking the way to Jericho (5:13–15). At first, he questioned this man: "Are you for us or for our enemies?" The answer was telling.

He was neither with Joshua nor with his enemies—this man was with the Lord and commanded the armies of the Lord. Now Joshua could be strong and courageous because he fully understood the Lord's promise to be with him always. True understanding dispels any doubt. And so in chapter 6, the Lord delivered Jericho into the hands of Joshua.

When Moses had approached these lands forty years before, the people did not understand that the Lord required them to be strong and courageous. They did not understand that the Lord promised to be with them always. They did not understand they should obey the Lord.

In the midst of this tale is the story of Rahab. She did not completely know this God, but she was willing to defy her king and make an open display of obedience. All she needed to understand was that this God was the true God. And it did not matter what the king or others in Jericho did or said. She displayed her allegiance to this God.

She knew something of God from the witness of

others. And she was willing to obey and join Him. She was ready to learn more and to trust her life to God. In so doing, she gained salvation for her entire family. And, as stated in verse 6:25, her salvation and the salvation of her family were rewarded forever. Discuss the level of understanding of Joshua, the Israelites, and Rahab.

Joshua understood enough and went boldly forward. Do we understand? What is it we need to understand? We certainly need to count the cost before making a commitment for our entire lives. But once we commit, we must be outward in our witness. We need to be courageous and strong—courageous and strong in our knowledge and understanding of the scriptures and of God.

Part of our counting the cost is to study and learn about God and our relationship. We need to know God and know ourselves. We must be able to defend our witness through intelligent response, and this requires us to understand the scriptures. We must be able to defend our witness through empathy, and this requires us to reflect on our life experiences.

The Question Again

Trusting and understanding comes with experience and with reason. It has been said that the best predictor of future behavior is relevant past behavior. To be able to rely on someone requires that we gain understanding of that person's tendencies and behavioral patterns through experience. Thus, we can learn of this requirement to trust God through experience with Him.

An example of these concepts can be found in the story of Balaam and the donkey (Numbers 22–24). Balaam was summoned by a ruler to curse Israel. Balaam stated that he could only pronounce what God led him to say, and he refused to go. After much pleading (and bribing), he was finally directed to go to the ruler. Balaam was about to pursue an ill-advised plan of action. As he rode his donkey, the donkey refused to proceed. This animal had always been trustworthy and obedient. But now he refused to go forward.

Balaam proceeded to beat the donkey because he refused to obey. This occurred three times. Finally, the donkey asked Balaam why he was being beaten. Had he ever disobeyed in the past? Had he ever led Balaam into harm's way? Why would Balaam assume the present action was obstinacy? He had no prior experience that would lead him to believe the donkey had any motive other than their common well-being.

Eventually Balaam is shown that it was only the donkey's action that saved his life. As strange as this story sounds, it points out that Balaam's action was baseless. In the end, he was shown that he should trust his prior experience with the donkey rather than just being willful.

If we carefully study the experiences of the people in scriptures, we can understand how to react to our circumstances. If we carefully reflect on our own life experiences, we can draw strength for the present and in the future. (The best way to learn is from the experience of others. But this is rarely done. The next best way to learn is from our own experiences.)

Each time we survive a minor tribulation, we should take stock of our strengths and weaknesses. We should learn that as dark as things seemed, we managed to pass on through and get stronger. From each life experience, we should grow in character and wisdom. If you have been in dire circumstances and survived, why do you doubt your ability to pass through this next circumstance?

After the incident has been resolved, we can often see that it was not as dreadful as we had imagined. If we truly trust God and His motivation, why do we question Him in the present instance? Are we so sure that we are in charge that we would rather beat God than trust Him?

The prayer of tranquility is particularly apt. We need to work hard to improve our situation and the situation of our families and communities. But we need to persevere and trust when presented with circumstances beyond our control. We need to remember that this life is important, but it is not the final act in the relationship with God. As important as this life is, it is only a prelude to the next existence. And it is important for others that we relate our life stories and witness. You may not know when something you say or do has a significant impact on someone else.

A Bible Answer: A Witness with Wisdom and Understanding

Just as God told Abraham, Jesus told the disciples that He would explain things to them (Genesis 18:17). They traveled together as He ministered for three years. He told them that slaves are to blindly obey, but friends are made aware of each other's thoughts, desires, and motivations. As Jesus ministered across the regions, His disciples observed and listened. And when they were alone, Jesus took the time to explain things as best they could understand at the time

(John 14:1–14, and chapter 16). He explained events, and He explained His parables.

When He performed miracles and boldly interacted with people of all stations of society, Jesus explained that they were to watch, learn, and then witness. After some time, Jesus gave His followers specific instructions on how to take His message to others on their own. They returned to report on all they had done and seen. And they received feedback from their teacher. This was a very purposeful indoctrination and guidance on how to venture out on their own based on the experience of having lived with their teacher (Matthew 10, Mark 6, Luke 9:1–9, and Luke 10:1–25).

Later, when the disciples had more experience and had witnessed the resurrection, Jesus could make clearer the relationship between them and the meaning of their history as recorded in their scriptures (the Old Testament). At the Last Supper, when He gave them the example of servant leadership by washing their feet, He told them, "You do not realize now what I am doing, but later you will understand." And, when He had finished, He asked, "Do you understand what I have done for you?" He went on to explain the meaning of "Teacher and Lord." He explained the relationship between God and His people. He explained that if they emulated the behavior they saw in Jesus, God would be pleased (John 13:1–17).

Then, on the road to Emmaus, He opened their eyes to the understanding of all that was written in the scriptures (Luke 24:13–35). With this experience and greater understanding, they could now witness to others what they had seen. It is not possible to properly witness without a level of understanding that comes with real-life experience and reasoned study and reflection.

When Jesus was being questioned by the high priest, He told them that He had spoken openly (John 18:19–24). There were many witnesses to what He had said. At this, an official struck Him in the face. Just as Balaam's donkey, Jesus asked why He was being struck. He said if anything He had spoken was untrue, to tell Him what it was. The truth can be deduced with reason combined with experience and the testimony of witnesses.

Small Group Outline

Discuss: Do you understand?

Scripture Reading: Joshua 1–6:25

What is it that we need to understand?

Discuss the need to count the cost before making a major commitment.

Discuss the need to seek knowledge as a way to understand the cost.

Discuss the need to understand ourselves.

Notes:

Scripture Reading: Numbers 22–24

Think about people who have had an impact on your life. Do they sometimes not realize that they have said or done something to impact you this way?

Discuss with the group times when people have told you that you made an impact on them without your realizing it.

Notes:

Scripture Reading: Luke 24:13–35; John 13:1–17

Do you recall being able to face difficult situations because you had previously faced less difficult situations?

Discuss how Jesus connected His life example with the Old Testament scriptures on the road to Emmaus as a means of giving His disciples greater understanding.

Discuss the lesson contained in the actions of Jesus during His last few days with His disciples.

Discuss the relationship between faith and knowledge.

How does one's faith become stronger with experience?

Notes:

CHAPTER 5

WHAT WILL GOD DO?

Is anything too hard for the Lord?
—Genesis 18:14

Scripture Reading: Genesis 18–24

The Bible Question

By his old age, Abraham had had many dealings
with God and his neighbors. He was prosperous, but
he still lacked a son with Sarah. God had promised
them a son, and Abraham and Sarah took it upon
themselves to have a surrogate son with Sarah's
Egyptian servant, as was a custom of the times. Not
knowing what God would do, they leaned on their

own understanding. And so in chapter 18 three visitors appeared over the horizon. Recognizing these as messengers from God, and obeying the rules of hospitality to strangers, Abraham begged them to stay and partake of his food and shelter.

As the preparations were made, the Lord asked, "Where is your wife, Sarah?" When the Lord proclaimed that they would have their promised child that year, Sarah again doubted (Genesis 18:12). And so the Lord continued, "Is anything too hard for the Lord?" (Genesis 18:13b). And so we see the interplay between God's promise and man's attempt to control events. God will stand by His promises.

And God will not leave people without understanding. In the next section of this chapter is an important dialogue. The Lord asked, "Shall I hide from Abraham what I am about to do?" (Genesis 18:17). There is first a clarification of the role of the descendants of Abraham and how this relates to world salvation. In verses 18–19, God repeated that He had chosen Abraham and would direct his children to keep the way of the Lord by doing what is right and just. This is the message in Scriptures from beginning to end.

Next there ensues a discussion of the fate of Sodom and Gomorrah (Genesis 18:20–33). It is a telling dialogue on the subject of judgment and mercy. Chapter 19 shows us the effort to save the righteous. It requires people to have faith, but with understanding based on experience.

As we have seen in prior chapters, we need not fear God. Yes, God is holy and righteous, but He also deals with people with understanding, mercy, and grace. As we learn of God's love, our response must be to show empathy as we strive to live in community—the God of love and grace coupled with Golden Rule.

Thus, this interaction between Abraham and the angels is very telling, but I want to focus on the claim that God does not hide what He will do (Genesis 18:16). In the early chapters of Genesis, while Adam and Eve were in the garden, there were two special trees identified that God had placed for the central purposes of their relationship. Only from the Tree of Knowledge must they not eat.

As indicated earlier, partaking of this knowledge led Adam to assume a legalistic view of their relationship with God. All along, life eternal was available to them as a gift from God. But with this legalistic view, rather than being guided by love and mercy, Adam cowered in fear before the power of God. Thus, God blocked Adam and Eve from gaining salvation through works, i.e. by eating of the Tree of Life. Instead, He clothed them with animal skins and sent them on their way.

God is the same from beginning to the end, but Adam and Eve had demonstrated that they did not truly know God—they did not understand mercy and grace. God must provide access to the Tree of Life in such a manner that people can see through their fear of God and finally understand God's love and grace. *He must willingly hang on that tree Himself.*

We need to see the payment for sin on the cross (judgment), but most important, we need to see that

God is willing to take this punishment on Himself. Once we understand the selflessness of true love (that God loves us enough to go to the cross in place of us), then we can truly comprehend that *we can always approach God with the confidence of a child approaching his beloved father.*

The Question Again

In the book of 1 Kings are the stories of the prophet Elijah. In 1 Kings 18, Elijah battled the false prophets in front of King Ahab. Elijah boldly challenged these prophets in the name of God. He urged them on and berated them with considerable trash talk. Finally, there was lightning and fire hurled down with much drama and bloodshed. This is our image of the God of the Old Testament. This is an image that evokes fear in people. This Elijah reminds me of the actions of someone who is fired with the brashness, passion, and vigor of youth.

Reading of this episode, one would imagine Elijah would fear no one. But, when confronted by Jezebel,

Elijah was fearful and exhausted. For all of his bluster, he could not maintain this level of fervor. Is this the fiery Elijah realizing that his actions were the brashness of inexperience? Was all of the fire and brimstone he witnessed not as significant as he had anticipated? Was he still unsure of God?

And so he fled in terror. Elijah fled as fast and hard as he was able. While fleeing, he was cared for and fed by birds. But on he traveled, farther away from his responsibilities. Finally, far away and hiding in a cave, Elijah wanted to hear God (1 Kings 19). He needed to rekindle his youthful vigor and brashness, but he was uncertain.

Did he not truly hear God when it rained down fire while battling the false prophets? Elijah's view of God, like our view of the Old Testament God, was distorted. Focusing on legalism, we fear God's awesome power. Reading the stories of the Old Testament, we are awestruck by the might. But is this an accurate and complete image of our awesome God?

How many times have people blamed God for the destruction of natural disasters? Tellingly, Elijah could not hear God in the great wind or the earthquake. He expected a God who demonstrated awesome power through mighty acts. But he could not hear God. Expecting a mighty pronouncement, Elijah sought a God of fire and brimstone.

But it was only in the gentle breeze that he heard the voice of God whisper to him. And while hiding from Jezebel, what message did Elijah receive from God? God asked Elijah, "What are you doing here?" Elijah was tired and fearful. He confessed that he was alone in fighting for God. At this, God corrected his shortsightedness. God knew there was more that Elijah did not see. God recounted that there were others on whom Elijah could rely. And God reminded Elijah that He was indeed with him. So Elijah needed to return to the people and bear witness without fear. *So God sent him back, refreshed and with renewed assurance.*

Our image of God may be power, fire, and brimstone.

Yet what we need is the God of peace, comfort, assurance, and joy, contained in the whisper of the gentle breeze. And so what will God do? He will consistently be God—He will not change.

A Bible Answer—The Assurance of the Presence of God

In Micah, the prophet speaks of a time when everyone will live without fear of their neighbors. This comes with an assurance of the presence of God. In Micah 4, God summarizes His plan for His people. People everywhere will see the presence of the Lord, and everyone will learn His ways.

Most of the Gospels deal with the last week in the life of Jesus. This is obviously a most important aspect of His life lesson. We started this study examining Adam's fear. From the beginning, God knew of the need for justice, but He also knew of the fear with which people live. And the only way to have the community of people understand the grace and love of God, and so to overcome this fear, was for the community to witness a God willing to take on the ultimate punishment for His people: the willing sacrifice of His only Son.

The many lessons in the Old Testament of substitution punishment for sin were meant to prepare us to understand and recognize Jesus and His role on the cross. We are especially struck by the lesson of Abraham willing to sacrifice his only son, only to realize that God will provide the sacrifice.

Jesus said that He must go to prepare a place for the disciples because this life is not all there is (John 18 and 19). When the authorities came to arrest Him, He asked, "Who is it you want?" (John 18:4). And he told Peter, "Shall I not drink from the cup the Father has given me?" (John 18:11).

Jesus must show everyone that God so loves His children that He is more than willing to do anything to show them that love. And, as He was questioned by the priests, Jesus asked them, "Why question me?" (Verse 18:21). He stated clearly that He had spoken openly for all to hear. They only needed to ask those who witnessed His actions. When the disciples were most fearful and confused, Jesus promised them that, in spite of His departure to the cross, He would always be with them.

The disciples were fearful when a fierce storm imperiled the boat, but Jesus was there. He chastised them for a lack of understanding of God that restricted their ability to face the storm with assurance. He then calmed the storm. And, by His presence, I am sure that He calmed their hearts (Matthew 8:23–27).

We all long for a life of peace without fear. We fear the unknown, we fear disease, we fear disaster, and we fear death. After the resurrection, the disciples would no longer fear death. While there were still many unknowns, they finally knew God. And God would always be there. While hardships still came their way, they now had the assurance of knowing that Jesus had spoken with true authority. This peace comes with knowing how much God cares about you—remember the cross and what He has done.

When people asked Billy Graham how he was able to always go forward with hope and joy, he responded, "I've read the last page of the Bible. It's all going to turn out all right."[3]

[3] Graham, Billy, *Life Wisdom from Billy Graham.* Hallmark Books, 2006.

Small Group Outline

Discuss: What will God do?

Scripture Reading: Genesis 18–24

Discuss our reaction to God's power when good things happen.

Discuss our reaction to God's power when bad things happen.

Discuss the meaning of *blessings* as good happenings. Reflect on being blessed as God looking on us favorably in both good times and bad times.

Notes:

Scripture Reading: 1 Kings 18:16–19:21

Discuss the image of God as all-powerful.

Discuss our understanding of God when faced with disease or natural disaster.

Discuss our understanding of nature and natural law contrasted with our expectation of miracles.

Discuss the difference between joy and happiness.

Notes:

Scripture Reading: John 18–19; Matthew 8:23–27

Contrast the disciples as described in the Gospels with the disciples as described in Acts and in the Epistles. What changed for the disciples?

How was the joy and boldness of the disciples the result of an assurance about God rather than the result of their circumstance?

Describe how you would react to circumstances without the assurance of knowing God is with you.

Notes:

CHAPTER 6

HOW WILL YOU RESPOND?

"Why are you angry?"
—Genesis 4:6

"If you do what is right, will you not be accepted?"
—Genesis 4:7

"Where is your brother?"
—Genesis 4:9

Scripture Reading: Genesis 4:1–26

The Bible Question

There are many times in the scriptures when someone is called by God. We have discussed Gideon, Moses, and several others in this study. We have seen people in the scriptures communing and worshiping with God. Right near the beginning of Genesis, we see the oldest child of Adam and Eve, Cain, working the soil (farming), and his younger sibling, Abel, tending the herds. From the text and the way this is portrayed, it seems as though Cain and Abel talked with God on a regular basis. And both brought offerings to Him.

Somehow (we are not told how) Cain believed that his offering was not favored by God, while Abel's offering was favored. Many sermons have been preached on why this was so. Maybe Cain presented some inferior portion rather than the first fruits of his harvest (see Genesis 4:3 "some of the fruits …").

I believe that perhaps this feeling of not being appreciated was only perception on the part of Cain. I believe God is pleased whenever people take the time to commune with Him and with His people. God is pleased that we care for one another as He cares for us. Whatever the reason, Cain believed that he sensed God's displeasure; Cain was more than out of sorts. He resented his perceived position in this world relative to that of his brother.

And so God posed questions that are implied throughout the entire scripture that we must all answer: "Why are you angry?" and "If you do what is right, will you not be accepted?" God explained to Cain that this anger and his perception of favoritism would lead to no good. Discuss these questions and statements.

So while God was focused on what was best for Cain, Cain was focused on how he was being improperly judged relative to Abel. We hear the Psalmist asking why the evil ones are doing well while we suffer. Why was Cain trying to discern God's reaction to Abel's offering? Should he not have been concerned with doing right? Instead of improving himself and judging his own progress, Cain became angry with Abel. God warned Cain that dwelling on his position relative to Abel rather than just striving to do good would lead to calamity and sin.

Cain deliberately killed Abel. Thus, God must ask

Cain the question we all remember, a question eerily similar to what was asked of Adam and Eve before: "Where is your brother?"

Cain's response is also similar to the answer given by Adam and Eve: "Am I my brother's keeper?" And the answer is a resounding, *yes*.

I believe Cain's main sin was to focus on his position relative to Abel as he perceived it. Cain was judging their merit rather than leaving judgment to God. Cain was focused on having more than his brother. Rather than focus on doing his best and doing good works, he was consumed by jealousy. This jealousy led Cain to tear down his brother in anger as his means of raising himself.

Cain realized too late what he had lost. Cain believed he would receive the judgment of death. Just like Adam and Eve, Cain understood the need for justice, but he did not comprehend mercy. Cain's punishment was to no longer live in the presence of the Lord (Genesis 4:10–14). But, even in his disobedience, God was still concerned for him. God placed an outwardly visible mark on Cain as one of God's people. Is this mark a foretelling of circumcision?

And so in this early story of the book of Genesis, so filled with dysfunctional people and families, God has a people. And as it states in verse 26b: "At that time men began to call on the name of the Lord." And so, what will you do? Will you compare yourself with others or will you serve others? If you are to compare yourself with others, isn't Jesus the plumb line, the standard against which we are all to be compared?

The Question Again

Read the book of Jonah. Jonah was given the task of warning a city. Jonah assumed the warning was a prelude to their punishment. He did not assume the warning was so that they could repent and be saved. Jonah refused to go to such a wicked city. They certainly would not listen. They were not worth the effort. They might even kill him. This attitude endangered the city needing God's message.

As Jonah fled in a boat, his actions subsequently endangered the boat's crew and all its passengers.

Realizing his flight was in vain, Jonah reluctantly delivered God's message. And miraculously, the city repented. Was their repentance sincere and lasting or was it just a safe reaction? (It was much like Pascal's gamble: Pascal stated that if there is no God, belief or not has no consequence. If there is a God and one disavows God, he is in jeopardy. So the safest odds are to accept a belief in God.)

And so when all the people of Nineveh repented, Jonah got upset with God because His prophesy did not go the way Jonah wanted (Jonah 4). Jonah was angry with God because God was merciful. Are we to be like Jonah and judge the response of others and God by how we think the world should respond to us?

As Jonah sulked by the side of the road, God decided to teach him (and us) a lesson in mercy. God provided a vine to shade Jonah from the hot sun. And Jonah continued to sulk. So then the vine died, and Jonah sulked more. So God once again asked questions of Jonah: "Do you have a right to be angry about the vine?" Jonah did nothing to grow the vine and yet was angry when it died. And then finally there was the question, "Should (God) not be concerned about (his people)?"

How often do we want mercy for ourselves but justice for others? (See Jonah 4:10–11.) Shouldn't God care and be merciful to whomever He chooses? If He is Lord, who are we to judge His ways? (See the parable of the king's debtor. Matthew 18:21–35)

A Bible Answer—The Servant and Steward

We are often angry at our suffering and at mercy to others. We are hard to please. But we *are* our brother's keepers, and we are to serve because we have been given so much. We *are* our brother's keepers because we know what it is to suffer. After the resurrection, Jesus asked Peter if he loved Him. With each positive reply, Jesus commanded him to serve others as the true response (John 21:15–17).

We are to witness with our actions, not just with our words and promises.

Consider the New Testament scriptures Matthew 14:13–21. We need to act justly and with mercy, but can we also not be so easily offended by the actions and words of others? In these verses, we tend to focus on the miracles of healings and feeding the thousands with a few loaves and fish. But what was the mood of Jesus on this day?

In this episode, Jesus was just told that His cousin, John the Baptist, had been beheaded by King Herod. Jesus and John had been close since before they were born. As stated in Luke 1:39–41: "At that time Mary got ready and hurried to a town in the hill country of Judea, where she entered Zechariah's house and greeted Elizabeth. When Elizabeth heard Mary's greeting, the baby [John] leaped in her womb, and Elizabeth was filled with the Holy Spirit."

So since childhood, Jesus and John probably spent considerable time together. I assume that the families were together several times a year when Mary and

Joseph came to Jerusalem for the feasts (Leviticus 23 and Luke 2:41). And it was Cousin John who baptized Jesus at the outset of His ministry. Close followers of John joined Jesus early in His ministry to assist Him and to study His teachings. Jesus and John were probably very close for thirty years and loved each other on many levels.

I believe on hearing of John's grisly death—a foretaste of His own future death—Jesus was quite sad and in a very grievous mood. He understandably just wanted to go off and be alone. But others made demands—selfish demands—on Him. Should not Jesus have the right to lash out in His grief and snap at them, "Can't you see I'm hurting? Just leave Me alone?" But instead, Jesus reacted by serving the needs of these people.

Surely Jesus was hurting because of the death of John, but it was not about His feelings. "The first question which the priest and the Levite asked was: 'If I stop to help this man, what will happen to me?' But … the Good Samaritan reversed the question:

'If I do not stop to help this man, what will happen to him?'[4] The disciples were acting like the priest and the Levite. Jesus had to teach them to act like the Samaritan—with empathy. *We* need to *heal them*; *we* need to *feed them*. Remember when *you* needed healing; remember when *you* needed to be fed.

---

[4] Edited by James Washington, *Martin Luther King, Jr., I Have A Dream*. Harper San Francisco, 1992.

Small Group Outline

Scripture Reading: Genesis 4:1–26

Discuss: How will you respond?

Discuss our tendency to compare ourselves with others. How does this affect your internal joy?

Can we be content just knowing we are doing what is right? Are we our brother's keeper?

What does it mean that sin is crouching at the door?

Read and discuss Micah 6:8.

Notes:

Scripture Reading: Jonah

Discuss our desire for justice for others and mercy for ourselves.

Discuss how you feel when you see evil people prosper.

Does God have the right to be merciful?

Notes:

Scripture Reading: John 21:15–17 and Matthew 14:13–21

Reflect on your understanding of God.

Discuss how people will serve others because they are instructed to do so.

Discuss how people will serve others because they are so grateful for how God cares about them, personally.

Read and discuss John 13:34–35; Matthew 5:43–48; 1 Corinthians 13:4–7

Briefly reflect on the several questions raised by God that were discussed in this book. As a result of reflecting on these questions:

Do you see God differently?

Do you see yourself differently?

Notes:

Printed in the United States
By Bookmasters